"*Think before you ~~~~~~*
Read before you think."

– Fran Lebowitz

This log book belongs to:

_____

BOOK LIST

WRITE THE TITLE ON THE SPINE AND
COLOR IN WHEN YOU'VE READ IT

BOOK LIST

Book Titles	Genre	Rating
1		☆☆☆☆☆
2		☆☆☆☆☆
3		☆☆☆☆☆
4		☆☆☆☆☆
5		☆☆☆☆☆
6		☆☆☆☆☆
7		☆☆☆☆☆
8		☆☆☆☆☆
9		☆☆☆☆☆
10		☆☆☆☆☆
11		☆☆☆☆☆
12		☆☆☆☆☆
13		☆☆☆☆☆
14		☆☆☆☆☆
15		☆☆☆☆☆
16		☆☆☆☆☆
17		☆☆☆☆☆
18		☆☆☆☆☆
19		☆☆☆☆☆
20		☆☆☆☆☆
21		☆☆☆☆☆
22		☆☆☆☆☆
23		☆☆☆☆☆
24		☆☆☆☆☆
25		☆☆☆☆☆

Book Titles	Genre	Rating
26		☆☆☆☆☆
27		☆☆☆☆☆
28		☆☆☆☆☆
29		☆☆☆☆☆
30		☆☆☆☆☆
31		☆☆☆☆☆
32		☆☆☆☆☆
33		☆☆☆☆☆
34		☆☆☆☆☆
35		☆☆☆☆☆
36		☆☆☆☆☆
37		☆☆☆☆☆
38		☆☆☆☆☆
39		☆☆☆☆☆
40		☆☆☆☆☆
41		☆☆☆☆☆
42		☆☆☆☆☆
43		☆☆☆☆☆
44		☆☆☆☆☆
45		☆☆☆☆☆
46		☆☆☆☆☆
47		☆☆☆☆☆
48		☆☆☆☆☆
49		☆☆☆☆☆
50		☆☆☆☆☆

BOOK TITLES	GENRE	RATING
51		☆☆☆☆☆
52		☆☆☆☆☆
53		☆☆☆☆☆
54		☆☆☆☆☆
55		☆☆☆☆☆
56		☆☆☆☆☆
57		☆☆☆☆☆
58		☆☆☆☆☆
59		☆☆☆☆☆
60		☆☆☆☆☆
61		☆☆☆☆☆
62		☆☆☆☆☆
63		☆☆☆☆☆
64		☆☆☆☆☆
65		☆☆☆☆☆
66		☆☆☆☆☆
67		☆☆☆☆☆
68		☆☆☆☆☆
69		☆☆☆☆☆
70		☆☆☆☆☆
71		☆☆☆☆☆
72		☆☆☆☆☆
73		☆☆☆☆☆
74		☆☆☆☆☆
75		☆☆☆☆☆

Book Titles	Genre	Rating
76		☆☆☆☆☆
77		☆☆☆☆☆
78		☆☆☆☆☆
79		☆☆☆☆☆
80		☆☆☆☆☆
81		☆☆☆☆☆
82		☆☆☆☆☆
83		☆☆☆☆☆
84		☆☆☆☆☆
85		☆☆☆☆☆
86		☆☆☆☆☆
87		☆☆☆☆☆
88		☆☆☆☆☆
89		☆☆☆☆☆
90		☆☆☆☆☆
91		☆☆☆☆☆
92		☆☆☆☆☆
93		☆☆☆☆☆
94		☆☆☆☆☆
95		☆☆☆☆☆
96		☆☆☆☆☆
97		☆☆☆☆☆
98		☆☆☆☆☆
99		☆☆☆☆☆
100		☆☆☆☆☆

○ PAPERBACK   ○ HARDBACK   ○ EBOOK   ○ AUDIOBOOK

No. 1

BOOK TITLE

AUTHOR _____   FICTION ○   NON- FICTION ○

GENRE: _____   DATE STARTED: _____   DATE FINISDHED: _____

PLOT/SUMMARY _____

_____

_____

_____

SOURCE:

BOUGHT ○   LOANED ○

FROM: _____

MY FAVORITE CHARACTER WAS _____

_____

THINGS I LEARNED:

WHAT I LIKED ABOUT THIS BOOK

_____

_____

_____

_____

_____

MEMORABLE QUOTES _____

_____

MY RATING

MY REVIEW _____

_____

_____

No.

○ PAPERBACK ○ HARDBACK ○ EBOOK ○ AUDIOBOOK

BOOK TITLE

AUTHOR _____ FICTION ○ NON- FICTION ○

GENRE: _____ DATE STARTED: _____ DATE FINISDHED: _____

PLOT/SUMMARY _____
_____
_____
_____
_____

SOURCE:

BOUGHT ○ LOANED ○

FROM: _____

MY FAVORITE CHARACTER WAS _____
_____

THINGS I LEARNED:

WHAT I LIKED ABOUT THIS BOOK _____
_____
_____
_____

_____
_____

MEMORABLE QUOTES _____
_____
_____

MY RATING

MY REVIEW _____
_____
_____

○ PAPERBACK   ○ HARDBACK   ○ EBOOK   ○ AUDIOBOOK   No.

BOOK
TITLE

AUTHOR _____   FICTION ○ NON- FICTION ○

GENRE: DATE STARTED: DATE FINISDHED:

PLOT/SUMMARY _____

_____

_____

_____

MY FAVORITE CHARACTER WAS _____

_____

WHAT I LIKED ABOUT THIS BOOK _____

_____

_____

_____

MEMORABLE QUOTES _____

_____

_____

MY REVIEW _____

_____

_____

_____

SOURCE:

BOUGHT ○ LOANED ○

FROM: _____

THINGS I LEARNED:

_____

_____

_____

MY RATING

No. ○ PAPERBACK ○ HARDBACK ○ EBOOK ○ AUDIOBOOK

BOOK TITLE

AUTHOR ....   FICTION ○ NON- FICTION ○

GENRE: DATE STARTED: DATE FINISDHED:

PLOT/SUMMARY

SOURCE:

BOUGHT ○ LOANED ○

FROM: ....

MY FAVORITE CHARACTER WAS ....

THINGS I LEARNED:

WHAT I LIKED ABOUT THIS BOOK

MEMORABLE QUOTES

MY RATING

MY REVIEW

○ PAPERBACK   ○ HARDBACK   ○ EBOOK   ○ AUDIOBOOK   **No.**

BOOK
TITLE

AUTHOR _____   FICTION ○ NON- FICTION ○

GENRE: DATE STARTED: DATE FINISDHED:

PLOT/SUMMARY _____
_____
_____
_____
_____

SOURCE:

BOUGHT ○ LOANED ○

FROM: _____

MY FAVORITE CHARACTER WAS _____
_____

WHAT I LIKED ABOUT THIS BOOK _____
_____
_____

THINGS I LEARNED:
_____
_____
_____

MEMORABLE QUOTES _____
_____

MY RATING

MY REVIEW _____
_____
_____

No. ○ PAPERBACK ○ HARDBACK ○ EBOOK ○ AUDIOBOOK

BOOK TITLE

AUTHOR _____ FICTION ○ NON-FICTION ○

GENRE: DATE STARTED: DATE FINISDHED:

PLOT/SUMMARY _____

_____
_____
_____
_____

SOURCE:

BOUGHT ○ LOANED ○

FROM: _____

MY FAVORITE CHARACTER WAS _____

_____

WHAT I LIKED ABOUT THIS BOOK _____

_____
_____
_____

THINGS I LEARNED:

_____
_____
_____

MEMORABLE QUOTES _____

_____
_____

MY RATING

MY REVIEW _____

_____
_____

○ PAPERBACK   ○ HARDBACK   ○ EBOOK   ○ AUDIOBOOK   **NO.**

BOOK
TITLE

AUTHOR _____   FICTION ○ NON- FICTION ○

GENRE: _____   DATE STARTED: _____   DATE FINISDHED: _____

PLOT/SUMMARY _____
_____
_____
_____
_____

MY FAVORITE CHARACTER WAS _____
_____

WHAT I LIKED ABOUT THIS BOOK _____
_____
_____
_____

MEMORABLE QUOTES _____
_____
_____

MY REVIEW _____
_____
_____
_____

SOURCE:

BOUGHT ○ LOANED ○

FROM: _____

THINGS I LEARNED:
_____
_____
_____

MY RATING

No. ○ PAPERBACK   ○ HARDBACK   ○ EBOOK   ○ AUDIOBOOK

| BOOK TITLE |

AUTHOR _____   FICTION ○   NON- FICTION ○

GENRE: DATE STARTED: DATE FINISDHED:

PLOT/SUMMARY _____

SOURCE:

BOUGHT ○   LOANED ○

FROM: _ _ _ _ _ _ _ _

MY FAVORITE CHARACTER WAS _____

THINGS I LEARNED:

WHAT I LIKED ABOUT THIS BOOK _____

MEMORABLE QUOTES _____

MY RATING

MY REVIEW _____

○ PAPERBACK   ○ HARDBACK   ○ EBOOK   ○ AUDIOBOOK   No.

BOOK
TITLE

AUTHOR _____   FICTION ○ NON-FICTION ○

GENRE: _____   DATE STARTED: _____   DATE FINISDHED: _____

PLOT/SUMMARY _____
_____
_____
_____
_____

SOURCE:

BOUGHT ○ LOANED ○

FROM: _____

MY FAVORITE CHARACTER WAS _____
_____

THINGS I LEARNED:

WHAT I LIKED ABOUT THIS BOOK _____
_____
_____
_____

MEMORABLE QUOTES _____
_____
_____

MY RATING

MY REVIEW _____
_____
_____
_____

No. ○ PAPERBACK ○ HARDBACK ○ EBOOK ○ AUDIOBOOK

BOOK TITLE

AUTHOR _____ FICTION ○ NON- FICTION ○

GENRE: DATE STARTED: DATE FINISDHED:

PLOT/SUMMARY _____
_____
_____
_____
_____

SOURCE:

BOUGHT ○ LOANED ○

FROM: _____

MY FAVORITE CHARACTER WAS _____
_____

THINGS I LEARNED:
_____
_____
_____

WHAT I LIKED ABOUT THIS BOOK _____
_____
_____
_____

MEMORABLE QUOTES _____
_____
_____

MY RATING

MY REVIEW _____
_____
_____
_____

○ PAPERBACK　　○ HARDBACK　　○ EBOOK　　○ AUDIOBOOK　　No.

BOOK
TITLE

AUTHOR _____　FICTION ○　NON- FICTION ○

GENRE:　　　　DATE STARTED:　　　　DATE FINISDHED:

PLOT/SUMMARY _____
_____
_____
_____
_____

MY FAVORITE CHARACTER WAS _____
_____

WHAT I LIKED ABOUT THIS BOOK
_____
_____
_____

MEMORABLE QUOTES _____
_____
_____

MY REVIEW _____
_____
_____

SOURCE:

BOUGHT○　LOANED○

FROM: _____

THINGS I LEARNED:
_____
_____

MY RATING

No. ○ PAPERBACK ○ HARDBACK ○ EBOOK ○ AUDIOBOOK

BOOK TITLE

AUTHOR .... FICTION ○ NON-FICTION ○

GENRE: DATE STARTED: DATE FINISDHED:

PLOT/SUMMARY ....

....
....
....
....

SOURCE:

BOUGHT ○ LOANED ○

FROM: ....

MY FAVORITE CHARACTER WAS ....

....

WHAT I LIKED ABOUT THIS BOOK ....

....
....
....

THINGS I LEARNED:

....
....
....

MEMORABLE QUOTES ....

....
....

MY REVIEW ....

MY RATING

....
....

○ PAPERBACK   ○ HARDBACK   ○ EBOOK   ○ AUDIOBOOK   No.

BOOK TITLE

AUTHOR _____   FICTION ○   NON- FICTION ○

GENRE: DATE STARTED: DATE FINISDHED:

PLOT/SUMMARY _____
_____
_____
_____

SOURCE:

BOUGHT ○   LOANED ○

FROM: _ _ _ _ _ _ _ _

MY FAVORITE CHARACTER WAS _____
_____

THINGS I LEARNED:

WHAT I LIKED ABOUT THIS BOOK _____
_____
_____

_____
_____

MEMORABLE QUOTES _____
_____
_____

MY RATING

MY REVIEW _____
_____
_____

No. ○ PAPERBACK   ○ HARDBACK   ○ EBOOK   ○ AUDIOBOOK

BOOK TITLE

AUTHOR _____   FICTION ○ NON- FICTION ○

GENRE: DATE STARTED: DATE FINISDHED:

PLOT/SUMMARY _____
_____
_____
_____
_____

MY FAVORITE CHARACTER WAS _____
_____

WHAT I LIKED ABOUT THIS BOOK _____
_____
_____
_____

MEMORABLE QUOTES _____
_____
_____

MY REVIEW _____
_____
_____

SOURCE:

BOUGHT ○ LOANED ○

FROM: _____

THINGS I LEARNED:
_____
_____
_____
_____

MY RATING

○ PAPERBACK   ○ HARDBACK   ○ EBOOK   ○ AUDIOBOOK   No.

| BOOK TITLE |

AUTHOR ....   FICTION ○   NON- FICTION ○

GENRE: DATE STARTED: DATE FINISDHED:

PLOT/SUMMARY ....

....

....

....

....

MY FAVORITE CHARACTER WAS ....

....

WHAT I LIKED ABOUT THIS BOOK ....

....

....

....

MEMORABLE QUOTES ....

....

....

MY REVIEW ....

....

....

SOURCE:

BOUGHT ○   LOANED ○

FROM: ....

THINGS I LEARNED:

....

....

....

MY RATING

No.

○ PAPERBACK ○ HARDBACK ○ EBOOK ○ AUDIOBOOK

BOOK TITLE

AUTHOR _____ FICTION ○ NON-FICTION ○

GENRE: _____ DATE STARTED: _____ DATE FINISDHED: _____

PLOT/SUMMARY _____
_____
_____
_____
_____

SOURCE:

BOUGHT ○ LOANED ○

FROM: _ _ _ _ _ _ _

MY FAVORITE CHARACTER WAS _____
_____

THINGS I LEARNED:
_____
_____
_____
_____

WHAT I LIKED ABOUT THIS BOOK _____
_____
_____
_____

MEMORABLE QUOTES _____
_____

MY RATING

MY REVIEW _____
_____
_____
_____

○ PAPERBACK   ○ HARDBACK   ○ EBOOK   ○ AUDIOBOOK   No.

| BOOK TITLE |

AUTHOR ....   FICTION ○ NON- FICTION ○

GENRE: DATE STARTED: DATE FINISDHED:

PLOT/SUMMARY ....

SOURCE:

BOUGHT○ LOANED ○

FROM: ....

MY FAVORITE CHARACTER WAS ....

THINGS I LEARNED:

WHAT I LIKED ABOUT THIS BOOK ....

MEMORABLE QUOTES ....

MY RATING

MY REVIEW ....

No.

○ PAPERBACK   ○ HARDBACK   ○ EBOOK   ○ AUDIOBOOK

BOOK TITLE

AUTHOR _____   FICTION ○   NON- FICTION ○

GENRE: _____   DATE STARTED: _____   DATE FINISDHED: _____

PLOT/SUMMARY _____
_____
_____
_____
_____

MY FAVORITE CHARACTER WAS _____
_____

WHAT I LIKED ABOUT THIS BOOK _____
_____
_____
_____

MEMORABLE QUOTES _____
_____
_____

MY REVIEW _____
_____
_____

SOURCE:
BOUGHT ○   LOANED ○
FROM: _____

THINGS I LEARNED:
_____
_____
_____

MY RATING

○ PAPERBACK   ○ HARDBACK   ○ EBOOK   ○ AUDIOBOOK   **No.**

BOOK
TITLE

AUTHOR _____   FICTION ○   NON- FICTION ○

GENRE: DATE STARTED: DATE FINISDHED:

PLOT/SUMMARY _____
_____
_____
_____
_____

SOURCE:

BOUGHT ○   LOANED ○

FROM: _____

MY FAVORITE CHARACTER WAS _____
_____

THINGS I LEARNED:

WHAT I LIKED ABOUT THIS BOOK _____
_____
_____

MEMORABLE QUOTES _____
_____

MY RATING

MY REVIEW _____
_____

No.

○ PAPERBACK   ○ HARDBACK   ○ EBOOK   ○ AUDIOBOOK

BOOK
TITLE

AUTHOR ....   FICTION ○ NON- FICTION ○

GENRE: DATE STARTED: DATE FINISDHED:

PLOT/SUMMARY ....

SOURCE:

BOUGHT ○ LOANED ○

FROM: ....

MY FAVORITE CHARACTER WAS ....

THINGS I LEARNED:

WHAT I LIKED ABOUT THIS BOOK ....

MEMORABLE QUOTES ....

MY RATING

MY REVIEW ....

○ PAPERBACK ○ HARDBACK ○ EBOOK ○ AUDIOBOOK | No.

BOOK
TITLE

AUTHOR _____ FICTION ○ NON- FICTION ○

GENRE: _____ DATE STARTED: _____ DATE FINISDHED: _____

PLOT/SUMMARY _____
_____
_____
_____
_____
_____

MY FAVORITE CHARACTER WAS _____
_____

WHAT I LIKED ABOUT THIS BOOK _____
_____
_____
_____

MEMORABLE QUOTES _____
_____
_____

SOURCE:

BOUGHT ○ LOANED ○

FROM: _____

THINGS I LEARNED:
_____
_____
_____

MY RATING

MY REVIEW _____
_____

No. ○ PAPERBACK ○ HARDBACK ○ EBOOK ○ AUDIOBOOK

| BOOK TITLE |

AUTHOR _____ FICTION ○ NON- FICTION ○

GENRE: DATE STARTED: DATE FINISDHED:

PLOT/SUMMARY _____
_____
_____
_____
_____

SOURCE:

BOUGHT ○ LOANED ○

FROM: _____

MY FAVORITE CHARACTER WAS _____
_____

THINGS I LEARNED:

WHAT I LIKED ABOUT THIS BOOK _____
_____
_____
_____

_____
_____
_____

MEMORABLE QUOTES _____
_____
_____

MY REVIEW _____

MY RATING

_____
_____
_____

○ PAPERBACK   ○ HARDBACK   ○ EBOOK   ○ AUDIOBOOK   **NO.**

BOOK TITLE

AUTHOR _____   FICTION ○ NON- FICTION ○

GENRE: DATE STARTED: DATE FINISDHED:

PLOT/SUMMARY _____
_____
_____
_____
_____

SOURCE:

BOUGHT ○   LOANED ○

FROM: _____

MY FAVORITE CHARACTER WAS _____
_____

THINGS I LEARNED:

WHAT I LIKED ABOUT THIS BOOK _____
_____
_____
_____

_____
_____
_____

MEMORABLE QUOTES _____
_____
_____

MY RATING

MY REVIEW _____
_____
_____
_____

No.

○ PAPERBACK ○ HARDBACK ○ EBOOK ○ AUDIOBOOK

BOOK TITLE

AUTHOR .... FICTION ○ NON- FICTION ○

GENRE: DATE STARTED: DATE FINISDHED:

PLOT/SUMMARY ....

SOURCE:

BOUGHT ○ LOANED ○

FROM: ....

MY FAVORITE CHARACTER WAS ....

THINGS I LEARNED:

WHAT I LIKED ABOUT THIS BOOK ....

MEMORABLE QUOTES ....

MY REVIEW ....

MY RATING

○ PAPERBACK   ○ HARDBACK   ○ EBOOK   ○ AUDIOBOOK   No.

BOOK
TITLE

AUTHOR .... FICTION ○ NON- FICTION ○

GENRE: DATE STARTED: DATE FINISDHED:

PLOT/SUMMARY ....

....

....

....

....

SOURCE:

BOUGHT ○ LOANED ○

FROM: ....

MY FAVORITE CHARACTER WAS ....

....

THINGS I LEARNED:

WHAT I LIKED ABOUT THIS BOOK ....

....

....

....

....

MEMORABLE QUOTES ....

....

....

MY RATING

MY REVIEW ....

....

....

....

No.

○ PAPERBACK   ○ HARDBACK   ○ EBOOK   ○ AUDIOBOOK

BOOK TITLE

AUTHOR _____   FICTION ○ NON- FICTION ○

GENRE: _____   DATE STARTED: _____   DATE FINISDHED: _____

PLOT/SUMMARY
_____
_____
_____
_____

SOURCE:
BOUGHT ○ LOANED ○
FROM: _____

MY FAVORITE CHARACTER WAS _____
_____

THINGS I LEARNED:
_____
_____
_____
_____

WHAT I LIKED ABOUT THIS BOOK _____
_____
_____
_____

MEMORABLE QUOTES _____
_____
_____

MY RATING

MY REVIEW _____
_____
_____

○ PAPERBACK   ○ HARDBACK   ○ EBOOK   ○ AUDIOBOOK | NO.

BOOK
TITLE

AUTHOR _____   FICTION ○ NON- FICTION ○

GENRE: DATE STARTED: DATE FINISDHED:

PLOT/SUMMARY _____
_____
_____
_____
_____

SOURCE:

BOUGHT ○ LOANED ○

FROM: _____

MY FAVORITE CHARACTER WAS _____
_____

THINGS I LEARNED:

WHAT I LIKED ABOUT THIS BOOK _____
_____
_____
_____
_____

MEMORABLE QUOTES _____
_____
_____

MY RATING

MY REVIEW _____
_____
_____

NO. ○ PAPERBACK   ○ HARDBACK   ○ EBOOK   ○ AUDIOBOOK

BOOK TITLE

AUTHOR .... FICTION ○ NON- FICTION ○

GENRE: DATE STARTED: DATE FINISDHED:

PLOT/SUMMARY ....

....
....
....
....

SOURCE:

BOUGHT ○   LOANED ○

FROM: ....

MY FAVORITE CHARACTER WAS ....
....

THINGS I LEARNED:
....
....
....

WHAT I LIKED ABOUT THIS BOOK ....
....
....
....
....

MEMORABLE QUOTES ....
....
....

MY RATING

MY REVIEW ....
....
....

○ PAPERBACK   ○ HARDBACK   ○ EBOOK   ○ AUDIOBOOK   **No.**

BOOK
TITLE

AUTHOR .... FICTION ○ NON- FICTION ○

GENRE: _____ DATE STARTED: _____ DATE FINISDHED: _____

PLOT/SUMMARY ....
....
....
....

SOURCE:

BOUGHT ○   LOANED ○

FROM: ....

MY FAVORITE CHARACTER WAS ....
....

THINGS I LEARNED:

WHAT I LIKED ABOUT THIS BOOK ....
....
....
....

MEMORABLE QUOTES ....
....

MY RATING

MY REVIEW ....
....
....

No. ○ PAPERBACK ○ HARDBACK ○ EBOOK ○ AUDIOBOOK

BOOK TITLE

AUTHOR .... FICTION ○ NON-FICTION ○

GENRE: DATE STARTED: DATE FINISDHED:

PLOT/SUMMARY ....
....
....
....
....

SOURCE:

BOUGHT ○ LOANED ○

FROM: ....

MY FAVORITE CHARACTER WAS ....
....

WHAT I LIKED ABOUT THIS BOOK ....
....
....
....

THINGS I LEARNED:
....
....
....

MEMORABLE QUOTES ....
....
....

MY RATING

MY REVIEW ....
....
....

○ PAPERBACK   ○ HARDBACK   ○ EBOOK   ○ AUDIOBOOK   **No.**

BOOK
TITLE

AUTHOR ....   FICTION ○   NON- FICTION ○

GENRE: DATE STARTED: DATE FINISDHED:

PLOT/SUMMARY ....

SOURCE:

BOUGHT ○   LOANED ○

FROM: ....

MY FAVORITE CHARACTER WAS ....

THINGS I LEARNED:

WHAT I LIKED ABOUT THIS BOOK ....

MEMORABLE QUOTES ....

MY RATING

MY REVIEW ....

No. ○ PAPERBACK ○ HARDBACK ○ EBOOK ○ AUDIOBOOK

BOOK TITLE

AUTHOR .... FICTION ○ NON- FICTION ○

GENRE: DATE STARTED: DATE FINISDHED:

PLOT/SUMMARY ....

SOURCE:

BOUGHT ○ LOANED ○

FROM: ....

MY FAVORITE CHARACTER WAS ....

THINGS I LEARNED:

WHAT I LIKED ABOUT THIS BOOK ....

MEMORABLE QUOTES ....

MY RATING

MY REVIEW ....

○ PAPERBACK   ○ HARDBACK   ○ EBOOK   ○ AUDIOBOOK   No.

BOOK
TITLE

AUTHOR ....   FICTION ○   NON- FICTION ○

GENRE: DATE STARTED: DATE FINISDHED:

PLOT/SUMMARY ....
....
....
....
....

SOURCE:

BOUGHT ○   LOANED ○

FROM: ....

MY FAVORITE CHARACTER WAS ....
....

THINGS I LEARNED:

WHAT I LIKED ABOUT THIS BOOK ....
....
....
....

MEMORABLE QUOTES ....
....
....

MY RATING

MY REVIEW ....
....
....

No. ○ PAPERBACK   ○ HARDBACK   ○ EBOOK   ○ AUDIOBOOK

BOOK TITLE

AUTHOR _____   FICTION ○   NON-FICTION ○

GENRE: DATE STARTED: DATE FINISDHED:

PLOT/SUMMARY
_____
_____
_____
_____

SOURCE:

BOUGHT ○   LOANED ○

FROM: _____

MY FAVORITE CHARACTER WAS _____
_____

THINGS I LEARNED:
_____
_____
_____

WHAT I LIKED ABOUT THIS BOOK _____
_____
_____
_____

MEMORABLE QUOTES _____
_____
_____

MY REVIEW _____
_____
_____
_____

MY RATING

○ PAPERBACK ○ HARDBACK ○ EBOOK ○ AUDIOBOOK **No.**

BOOK
TITLE

AUTHOR .... FICTION ○ NON- FICTION ○

GENRE: DATE STARTED: DATE FINISDHED:

PLOT/SUMMARY ....
....
....
....
....

SOURCE:

BOUGHT ○ LOANED ○

FROM: ....

MY FAVORITE CHARACTER WAS ....
....

THINGS I LEARNED:

WHAT I LIKED ABOUT THIS BOOK ....
....
....
....

....
....
....

MEMORABLE QUOTES ....
....
....

MY RATING

MY REVIEW ....
....
....

No.

○ PAPERBACK   ○ HARDBACK   ○ EBOOK   ○ AUDIOBOOK

BOOK TITLE

AUTHOR _____   FICTION ○   NON- FICTION ○

GENRE: _____   DATE STARTED: _____   DATE FINISDHED: _____

PLOT/SUMMARY _____
_____
_____
_____
_____

MY FAVORITE CHARACTER WAS _____
_____

WHAT I LIKED ABOUT THIS BOOK _____
_____
_____
_____

MEMORABLE QUOTES _____
_____
_____

MY REVIEW _____
_____
_____

SOURCE:

BOUGHT ○   LOANED ○

FROM: _____

THINGS I LEARNED:
_____
_____
_____

MY RATING

○ PAPERBACK   ○ HARDBACK   ○ EBOOK   ○ AUDIOBOOK   No.

BOOK TITLE

AUTHOR _____   FICTION ○ NON- FICTION ○

GENRE: DATE STARTED: DATE FINISDHED:

PLOT/SUMMARY _____

_____
_____
_____
_____

SOURCE:

BOUGHT ○ LOANED ○

FROM: _____

MY FAVORITE CHARACTER WAS _____

_____

THINGS I LEARNED:

WHAT I LIKED ABOUT THIS BOOK _____

_____
_____
_____

_____
_____

MEMORABLE QUOTES _____

_____
_____

MY RATING

MY REVIEW _____

_____
_____
_____
_____

No.

○ PAPERBACK ○ HARDBACK ○ EBOOK ○ AUDIOBOOK

BOOK TITLE

AUTHOR _____ FICTION ○ NON-FICTION ○

GENRE: _____ DATE STARTED: _____ DATE FINISDHED: _____

PLOT/SUMMARY _____
_____
_____
_____
_____

MY FAVORITE CHARACTER WAS _____
_____

WHAT I LIKED ABOUT THIS BOOK _____
_____
_____

MEMORABLE QUOTES _____
_____
_____

MY REVIEW _____
_____
_____
_____

SOURCE:

BOUGHT ○ LOANED ○

FROM: _____

THINGS I LEARNED:
_____
_____
_____

MY RATING

○ PAPERBACK   ○ HARDBACK   ○ EBOOK   ○ AUDIOBOOK   No.

BOOK TITLE

AUTHOR ....   FICTION ○   NON- FICTION ○

GENRE: DATE STARTED: DATE FINISDHED:

PLOT/SUMMARY ....
....
....
....
....

SOURCE:

BOUGHT ○   LOANED ○

FROM: ....

MY FAVORITE CHARACTER WAS ....
....

THINGS I LEARNED:

WHAT I LIKED ABOUT THIS BOOK ....
....
....
....

MEMORABLE QUOTES ....
....
....

MY RATING

MY REVIEW ....
....
....

No. ○ PAPERBACK   ○ HARDBACK   ○ EBOOK   ○ AUDIOBOOK

BOOK TITLE

AUTHOR ....   FICTION ○ NON- FICTION ○

GENRE: DATE STARTED: DATE FINISDHED:

PLOT/SUMMARY ....

....

....

....

SOURCE:

BOUGHT ○ LOANED ○

FROM: ....

MY FAVORITE CHARACTER WAS ....

....

THINGS I LEARNED:

....

....

....

WHAT I LIKED ABOUT THIS BOOK ....

....

....

....

MEMORABLE QUOTES ....

....

....

MY RATING

MY REVIEW ....

....

....

○ PAPERBACK　　　○ HARDBACK　　　○ EBOOK　　　○ AUDIOBOOK　　**No.**

BOOK TITLE	

AUTHOR ....　　FICTION ○　NON- FICTION ○

GENRE: ....　DATE STARTED: ....　DATE FINISDHED: ....

PLOT/SUMMARY ....
....
....
....
....
....

SOURCE:

BOUGHT ○　LOANED ○

FROM: ....

MY FAVORITE CHARACTER WAS ....
....

THINGS I LEARNED:

....

WHAT I LIKED ABOUT THIS BOOK ....
....
....
....

MEMORABLE QUOTES ....
....
....

MY REVIEW ....
....
....
....

MY RATING

No. ○ PAPERBACK ○ HARDBACK ○ EBOOK ○ AUDIOBOOK

BOOK TITLE

AUTHOR _____ FICTION ○ NON- FICTION ○

GENRE: _____ DATE STARTED: _____ DATE FINISDHED: _____

PLOT/SUMMARY _____
_____
_____
_____
_____

SOURCE:

BOUGHT ○ LOANED ○

FROM: _ _ _ _ _ _ _ _ _

MY FAVORITE CHARACTER WAS _____
_____

WHAT I LIKED ABOUT THIS BOOK _____
_____
_____
_____

THINGS I LEARNED:
_____
_____
_____
_____

MEMORABLE QUOTES _____
_____
_____

MY RATING

MY REVIEW _____
_____
_____
_____

○ PAPERBACK   ○ HARDBACK   ○ EBOOK   ○ AUDIOBOOK   **No.**

BOOK TITLE

AUTHOR _____   FICTION ○ NON- FICTION ○

GENRE: DATE STARTED: DATE FINISDHED:

PLOT/SUMMARY _____

_____

_____

_____

SOURCE:

BOUGHT ○   LOANED ○

FROM: _____

MY FAVORITE CHARACTER WAS _____

_____

WHAT I LIKED ABOUT THIS BOOK _____

_____

_____

_____

THINGS I LEARNED:

_____

_____

MEMORABLE QUOTES _____

_____

_____

MY RATING

MY REVIEW _____

_____

_____

_____

No.

○ PAPERBACK   ○ HARDBACK   ○ EBOOK   ○ AUDIOBOOK

BOOK TITLE

AUTHOR _____   FICTION ○   NON- FICTION ○

GENRE: _____   DATE STARTED: _____   DATE FINISDHED: _____

PLOT/SUMMARY _____
_____
_____
_____
_____

SOURCE:

BOUGHT ○   LOANED ○

FROM: _____

MY FAVORITE CHARACTER WAS _____
_____

THINGS I LEARNED:

WHAT I LIKED ABOUT THIS BOOK _____
_____
_____
_____
_____

MEMORABLE QUOTES _____
_____
_____

MY RATING

MY REVIEW _____
_____
_____

○ PAPERBACK   ○ HARDBACK   ○ EBOOK   ○ AUDIOBOOK   NO.

BOOK
TITLE

AUTHOR _____   FICTION ○ NON- FICTION ○

GENRE: DATE STARTED: DATE FINISDHED:

PLOT/SUMMARY _____
_____
_____
_____
_____
_____

MY FAVORITE CHARACTER WAS _____
_____

WHAT I LIKED ABOUT THIS BOOK _____
_____
_____
_____

MEMORABLE QUOTES _____
_____
_____

MY REVIEW _____
_____

SOURCE:

BOUGHT ○   LOANED ○

FROM: _____

THINGS I LEARNED:
_____
_____
_____
_____

MY RATING

No.

○ PAPERBACK   ○ HARDBACK   ○ EBOOK   ○ AUDIOBOOK

BOOK TITLE

AUTHOR _____   FICTION ○ NON- FICTION ○

GENRE: _____   DATE STARTED: _____   DATE FINISDHED: _____

PLOT/SUMMARY _____
_____
_____
_____

MY FAVORITE CHARACTER WAS _____
_____

WHAT I LIKED ABOUT THIS BOOK _____
_____
_____
_____

MEMORABLE QUOTES _____
_____
_____

MY REVIEW _____
_____

SOURCE:

BOUGHT ○   LOANED ○

FROM: _____

THINGS I LEARNED:
_____
_____
_____

MY RATING

○ PAPERBACK ○ HARDBACK ○ EBOOK ○ AUDIOBOOK | **NO.**

BOOK
TITLE

AUTHOR .... FICTION ○ NON- FICTION ○

GENRE: DATE STARTED: DATE FINISDHED:

PLOT/SUMMARY ....

SOURCE:

BOUGHT ○ LOANED ○

FROM: ....

MY FAVORITE CHARACTER WAS ....

THINGS I LEARNED:

WHAT I LIKED ABOUT THIS BOOK ....

MEMORABLE QUOTES ....

MY RATING

MY REVIEW ....

No. ○ PAPERBACK ○ HARDBACK ○ EBOOK ○ AUDIOBOOK

BOOK TITLE

AUTHOR .... FICTION ○ NON- FICTION ○

GENRE: DATE STARTED: DATE FINISDHED:

PLOT/SUMMARY ....

SOURCE:

BOUGHT ○ LOANED ○

FROM: ....

MY FAVORITE CHARACTER WAS ....

THINGS I LEARNED:

WHAT I LIKED ABOUT THIS BOOK ....

MEMORABLE QUOTES ....

MY RATING

MY REVIEW ....

○ PAPERBACK   ○ HARDBACK   ○ EBOOK   ○ AUDIOBOOK   No.

BOOK
TITLE

AUTHOR _____   FICTION ○   NON- FICTION ○

GENRE: _____   DATE STARTED: _____   DATE FINISDHED: _____

PLOT/SUMMARY _____

_____

_____

_____

_____

SOURCE:

BOUGHT ○   LOANED ○

FROM: _____

MY FAVORITE CHARACTER WAS _____

_____

THINGS I LEARNED:

WHAT I LIKED ABOUT THIS BOOK _____

_____

_____

_____

_____

_____

_____

MEMORABLE QUOTES _____

_____

MY RATING

MY REVIEW _____

_____

_____

No. ○ PAPERBACK   ○ HARDBACK   ○ EBOOK   ○ AUDIOBOOK

| BOOK TITLE |

AUTHOR _____   FICTION ○ NON- FICTION ○

GENRE: DATE STARTED: DATE FINISDHED:

PLOT/SUMMARY _____

_____
_____
_____
_____

MY FAVORITE CHARACTER WAS _____
_____

WHAT I LIKED ABOUT THIS BOOK _____
_____
_____
_____

MEMORABLE QUOTES _____
_____
_____

MY REVIEW _____
_____
_____
_____

SOURCE:

BOUGHT ○ LOANED ○

FROM: _____

THINGS I LEARNED:
_____
_____
_____

MY RATING

○ PAPERBACK   ○ HARDBACK   ○ EBOOK   ○ AUDIOBOOK   **No.**

BOOK TITLE

AUTHOR _____   FICTION ○   NON-FICTION ○

GENRE: _____   DATE STARTED: _____   DATE FINISDHED: _____

PLOT/SUMMARY _____

_____

_____

_____

_____

SOURCE:

BOUGHT ○   LOANED ○

FROM: _____

MY FAVORITE CHARACTER WAS _____

_____

WHAT I LIKED ABOUT THIS BOOK _____

_____

_____

THINGS I LEARNED:

_____

_____

_____

MEMORABLE QUOTES _____

_____

MY RATING

MY REVIEW _____

_____

No.

○ PAPERBACK ○ HARDBACK ○ EBOOK ○ AUDIOBOOK

BOOK TITLE

AUTHOR _____ FICTION ○ NON- FICTION ○

GENRE: DATE STARTED: DATE FINISDHED:

PLOT/SUMMARY _____
_____
_____
_____
_____

SOURCE:

BOUGHT ○ LOANED ○

FROM: _____

MY FAVORITE CHARACTER WAS _____
_____

WHAT I LIKED ABOUT THIS BOOK _____
_____
_____
_____

THINGS I LEARNED:
_____
_____
_____

MEMORABLE QUOTES _____
_____
_____

MY RATING

MY REVIEW _____
_____
_____

○ PAPERBACK ○ HARDBACK ○ EBOOK ○ AUDIOBOOK **No.**

BOOK TITLE

AUTHOR .... FICTION ○ NON- FICTION ○

GENRE: DATE STARTED: DATE FINISDHED:

PLOT/SUMMARY ....

SOURCE:

BOUGHT ○ LOANED ○

FROM: ....

MY FAVORITE CHARACTER WAS ....

THINGS I LEARNED:

WHAT I LIKED ABOUT THIS BOOK

MEMORABLE QUOTES ....

MY RATING

MY REVIEW ....

No. ○ PAPERBACK　　○ HARDBACK　　○ EBOOK　　○ AUDIOBOOK

BOOK TITLE

AUTHOR _____　FICTION ○ NON- FICTION ○

GENRE:　　　　DATE STARTED:　　　　DATE FINISDHED:

PLOT/SUMMARY _____
_____
_____
_____
_____

MY FAVORITE CHARACTER WAS _____
_____

WHAT I LIKED ABOUT THIS BOOK _____
_____
_____
_____

MEMORABLE QUOTES _____
_____
_____

SOURCE:

BOUGHT ○　LOANED ○

FROM: _____

THINGS I LEARNED:
_____
_____
_____

MY RATING

MY REVIEW _____
_____
_____

○ PAPERBACK   ○ HARDBACK   ○ EBOOK   ○ AUDIOBOOK   No.

BOOK TITLE	

AUTHOR _____ FICTION ○ NON- FICTION ○

GENRE: DATE STARTED: DATE FINISDHED:

PLOT/SUMMARY _____

SOURCE:

BOUGHT ○   LOANED ○

FROM: _____

MY FAVORITE CHARACTER WAS _____

THINGS I LEARNED:

WHAT I LIKED ABOUT THIS BOOK _____

MEMORABLE QUOTES _____

MY RATING

MY REVIEW _____

No.

○ PAPERBACK ○ HARDBACK ○ EBOOK ○ AUDIOBOOK

BOOK TITLE

AUTHOR .... FICTION ○ NON- FICTION ○

GENRE: DATE STARTED: DATE FINISDHED:

PLOT/SUMMARY ....

....
....
....
....

SOURCE:

BOUGHT ○ LOANED ○

FROM: ....

MY FAVORITE CHARACTER WAS ....

....

THINGS I LEARNED:

....

WHAT I LIKED ABOUT THIS BOOK ....

....
....
....

MEMORABLE QUOTES ....

....
....

MY REVIEW ....

MY RATING

....
....
....

○ PAPERBACK   ○ HARDBACK   ○ EBOOK   ○ AUDIOBOOK   No.

BOOK TITLE

AUTHOR ....   FICTION ○ NON- FICTION ○

GENRE: DATE STARTED: DATE FINISDHED:

PLOT/SUMMARY ....

SOURCE:

BOUGHT ○   LOANED ○

FROM: ....

MY FAVORITE CHARACTER WAS ....

THINGS I LEARNED:

WHAT I LIKED ABOUT THIS BOOK

MEMORABLE QUOTES ....

MY RATING

MY REVIEW ....

No.

○ PAPERBACK ○ HARDBACK ○ EBOOK ○ AUDIOBOOK

BOOK TITLE

AUTHOR .... FICTION ○ NON- FICTION ○

GENRE: DATE STARTED: DATE FINISDHED:

PLOT/SUMMARY ....

SOURCE:

BOUGHT ○ LOANED ○

FROM: ....

MY FAVORITE CHARACTER WAS ....

THINGS I LEARNED:

WHAT I LIKED ABOUT THIS BOOK ....

MEMORABLE QUOTES ....

MY RATING

MY REVIEW ....

○ PAPERBACK   ○ HARDBACK   ○ EBOOK   ○ AUDIOBOOK   No.

BOOK
TITLE

AUTHOR ....   FICTION ○   NON- FICTION ○

GENRE: DATE STARTED: DATE FINISDHED:

PLOT/SUMMARY ....

....

....

....

SOURCE:

BOUGHT ○   LOANED ○

FROM: ....

MY FAVORITE CHARACTER WAS ....

....

THINGS I LEARNED:

WHAT I LIKED ABOUT THIS BOOK ....

....

....

....

....

MEMORABLE QUOTES ....

....

MY RATING

MY REVIEW ....

....

....

....

No.

○ PAPERBACK   ○ HARDBACK   ○ EBOOK   ○ AUDIOBOOK

| BOOK TITLE |

AUTHOR _____   FICTION ○ NON- FICTION ○

GENRE: _____   DATE STARTED: _____   DATE FINISDHED: _____

PLOT/SUMMARY
_____
_____
_____
_____

MY FAVORITE CHARACTER WAS _____
_____

WHAT I LIKED ABOUT THIS BOOK _____
_____
_____
_____

MEMORABLE QUOTES _____
_____

MY REVIEW
_____
_____
_____

SOURCE:

BOUGHT ○   LOANED ○

FROM: _____

THINGS I LEARNED:
_____
_____
_____

MY RATING

☹ 😐 🙂

★ ★ ★
★ ★ ★

○ PAPERBACK   ○ HARDBACK   ○ EBOOK   ○ AUDIOBOOK   No.

BOOK
TITLE

AUTHOR .... FICTION ○ NON- FICTION ○

GENRE: DATE STARTED: DATE FINISDHED:

PLOT/SUMMARY ....

SOURCE:

BOUGHT ○ LOANED ○

FROM: ....

MY FAVORITE CHARACTER WAS ....

THINGS I LEARNED:

WHAT I LIKED ABOUT THIS BOOK ....

MEMORABLE QUOTES ....

MY RATING

MY REVIEW ....

No.

○ PAPERBACK   ○ HARDBACK   ○ EBOOK   ○ AUDIOBOOK

| BOOK TITLE |

AUTHOR ....   FICTION ○ NON- FICTION ○

GENRE: DATE STARTED: DATE FINISDHED:

PLOT/SUMMARY ....

MY FAVORITE CHARACTER WAS ---------------------------

WHAT I LIKED ABOUT THIS BOOK ------------------------

MEMORABLE QUOTES ----------------------------------

MY REVIEW

SOURCE:

BOUGHT ○ LOANED ○

FROM: ----------

THINGS I LEARNED:

MY RATING

○ PAPERBACK   ○ HARDBACK   ○ EBOOK   ○ AUDIOBOOK   **NO.**

BOOK
TITLE

AUTHOR ....   FICTION ○   NON- FICTION ○

GENRE: _____   DATE STARTED: _____   DATE FINISDHED: _____

PLOT/SUMMARY ....

SOURCE:

BOUGHT ○   LOANED ○

FROM: _____

MY FAVORITE CHARACTER WAS ....

THINGS I LEARNED:

WHAT I LIKED ABOUT THIS BOOK ....

MEMORABLE QUOTES ....

MY RATING

MY REVIEW ....

No. ○ PAPERBACK   ○ HARDBACK   ○ EBOOK   ○ AUDIOBOOK

BOOK TITLE

AUTHOR _____   FICTION ○ NON- FICTION ○

GENRE: DATE STARTED: DATE FINISDHED:

PLOT/SUMMARY _____

_____

_____

_____

_____

SOURCE:

BOUGHT ○   LOANED ○

FROM: _____

MY FAVORITE CHARACTER WAS _____

_____

THINGS I LEARNED:

WHAT I LIKED ABOUT THIS BOOK _____

_____

_____

_____

_____

MEMORABLE QUOTES _____

_____

_____

MY RATING

MY REVIEW _____

_____

_____

_____

○ PAPERBACK   ○ HARDBACK   ○ EBOOK   ○ AUDIOBOOK   **No.**

BOOK TITLE

AUTHOR _____   FICTION ○   NON- FICTION ○

GENRE: _____   DATE STARTED: _____   DATE FINISDHED: _____

PLOT/SUMMARY _____

_____

_____

_____

_____

SOURCE:

BOUGHT ○   LOANED ○

FROM: _____

MY FAVORITE CHARACTER WAS _____

_____

THINGS I LEARNED:

WHAT I LIKED ABOUT THIS BOOK _____

_____

_____

_____

_____

_____

MEMORABLE QUOTES _____

_____

MY RATING

MY REVIEW _____

_____

_____

_____

No. ○ PAPERBACK ○ HARDBACK ○ EBOOK ○ AUDIOBOOK

BOOK TITLE

AUTHOR _____ FICTION ○ NON- FICTION ○

GENRE: DATE STARTED: DATE FINISDHED:

PLOT/SUMMARY _____
_____
_____
_____
_____

MY FAVORITE CHARACTER WAS _____
_____

WHAT I LIKED ABOUT THIS BOOK _____
_____
_____
_____

MEMORABLE QUOTES _____
_____
_____

MY REVIEW _____
_____
_____

SOURCE:

BOUGHT ○ LOANED ○

FROM: _____

THINGS I LEARNED:
_____
_____
_____

MY RATING

○ PAPERBACK   ○ HARDBACK   ○ EBOOK   ○ AUDIOBOOK   No.

BOOK TITLE

AUTHOR .... FICTION ○ NON- FICTION ○

GENRE: ....   DATE STARTED: ....   DATE FINISDHED: ....

PLOT/SUMMARY ....

....

....

....

....

SOURCE:

BOUGHT ○ LOANED ○

FROM: ....

MY FAVORITE CHARACTER WAS ....

....

THINGS I LEARNED:

WHAT I LIKED ABOUT THIS BOOK ....

....

....

....

....

....

MEMORABLE QUOTES ....

....

MY RATING

MY REVIEW ....

....

....

No.

○ PAPERBACK ○ HARDBACK ○ EBOOK ○ AUDIOBOOK

BOOK TITLE

AUTHOR .... FICTION ○ NON- FICTION ○

GENRE: DATE STARTED: DATE FINISDHED:

PLOT/SUMMARY ....
....
....
....

SOURCE:

BOUGHT ○ LOANED ○

FROM: ....

MY FAVORITE CHARACTER WAS ....
....

THINGS I LEARNED:

WHAT I LIKED ABOUT THIS BOOK ....
....
....
....

MEMORABLE QUOTES ....
....
....

MY RATING

MY REVIEW ....
....
....

○ PAPERBACK ○ HARDBACK ○ EBOOK ○ AUDIOBOOK **No.**

BOOK TITLE

AUTHOR .... FICTION ○ NON-FICTION ○

GENRE: DATE STARTED: DATE FINISDHED:

PLOT/SUMMARY ....

SOURCE:

BOUGHT ○ LOANED ○

FROM: ....

MY FAVORITE CHARACTER WAS ....

THINGS I LEARNED:

WHAT I LIKED ABOUT THIS BOOK ....

MEMORABLE QUOTES ....

MY RATING

MY REVIEW ....

No.

○ PAPERBACK ○ HARDBACK ○ EBOOK ○ AUDIOBOOK

BOOK TITLE

AUTHOR _____ FICTION ○ NON- FICTION ○

GENRE: DATE STARTED: DATE FINISDHED:

PLOT/SUMMARY _____
_____
_____
_____
_____

MY FAVORITE CHARACTER WAS _____
_____

WHAT I LIKED ABOUT THIS BOOK _____
_____
_____
_____

MEMORABLE QUOTES _____
_____
_____

MY REVIEW _____
_____
_____

SOURCE:

BOUGHT ○ LOANED ○

FROM: _____

THINGS I LEARNED:
_____
_____
_____

MY RATING

○ PAPERBACK   ○ HARDBACK   ○ EBOOK   ○ AUDIOBOOK   No.

BOOK
TITLE

AUTHOR .... FICTION ○ NON-FICTION ○

GENRE: DATE STARTED: DATE FINISDHED:

PLOT/SUMMARY ....

SOURCE:

BOUGHT ○ LOANED ○

FROM: ....

MY FAVORITE CHARACTER WAS ....

THINGS I LEARNED:

WHAT I LIKED ABOUT THIS BOOK ....

MEMORABLE QUOTES ....

MY RATING

MY REVIEW ....

No. ○ PAPERBACK ○ HARDBACK ○ EBOOK ○ AUDIOBOOK

BOOK TITLE

AUTHOR .... FICTION ○ NON- FICTION ○

GENRE: DATE STARTED: DATE FINISDHED:

PLOT/SUMMARY ....

....

....

....

MY FAVORITE CHARACTER WAS ....

....

WHAT I LIKED ABOUT THIS BOOK ....

....

....

....

MEMORABLE QUOTES ....

....

....

MY REVIEW ....

....

....

SOURCE:

BOUGHT ○ LOANED ○

FROM: ....

THINGS I LEARNED:

....

....

....

MY RATING

○ PAPERBACK   ○ HARDBACK   ○ EBOOK   ○ AUDIOBOOK   **No.**

BOOK TITLE

AUTHOR .... FICTION ○ NON- FICTION ○

GENRE: DATE STARTED: DATE FINISDHED:

PLOT/SUMMARY

SOURCE:

BOUGHT ○   LOANED ○

FROM: ....

MY FAVORITE CHARACTER WAS

THINGS I LEARNED:

WHAT I LIKED ABOUT THIS BOOK

MEMORABLE QUOTES

MY RATING

MY REVIEW

No.

○ PAPERBACK ○ HARDBACK ○ EBOOK ○ AUDIOBOOK

BOOK TITLE

AUTHOR _____ FICTION ○ NON- FICTION ○

GENRE: DATE STARTED: DATE FINISDHED:

PLOT/SUMMARY _____
_____
_____
_____
_____

SOURCE:

BOUGHT ○ LOANED ○
FROM: _____

MY FAVORITE CHARACTER WAS _____
_____

WHAT I LIKED ABOUT THIS BOOK _____
_____
_____
_____

THINGS I LEARNED:
_____
_____
_____

MEMORABLE QUOTES _____
_____
_____

MY RATING

MY REVIEW _____
_____
_____

○ PAPERBACK   ○ HARDBACK   ○ EBOOK   ○ AUDIOBOOK   No.

BOOK
TITLE

AUTHOR ....   FICTION ○ NON-FICTION ○

GENRE: DATE STARTED: DATE FINISDHED:

PLOT/SUMMARY ....

....

....

....

....

SOURCE:

BOUGHT ○   LOANED ○

FROM: ....

MY FAVORITE CHARACTER WAS ....

....

THINGS I LEARNED:

WHAT I LIKED ABOUT THIS BOOK ....

....

....

....

....

MEMORABLE QUOTES ....

....

MY RATING

MY REVIEW ....

....

....

No.

○ PAPERBACK ○ HARDBACK ○ EBOOK ○ AUDIOBOOK

BOOK TITLE

AUTHOR _____ FICTION ○ NON- FICTION ○

GENRE: DATE STARTED: DATE FINISDHED:

PLOT/SUMMARY _____

_____
_____
_____
_____

MY FAVORITE CHARACTER WAS _____
_____

WHAT I LIKED ABOUT THIS BOOK _____
_____
_____
_____

MEMORABLE QUOTES _____
_____
_____

MY REVIEW
_____
_____
_____

SOURCE:

BOUGHT ○ LOANED ○
FROM: _____

THINGS I LEARNED:
_____
_____
_____
_____

MY RATING

○ PAPERBACK ○ HARDBACK ○ EBOOK ○ AUDIOBOOK No.

BOOK TITLE

AUTHOR .... FICTION ○ NON- FICTION ○

GENRE: DATE STARTED: DATE FINISDHED:

PLOT/SUMMARY ....

....

....

....

SOURCE:

BOUGHT ○ LOANED ○

FROM: ....

MY FAVORITE CHARACTER WAS ....

....

THINGS I LEARNED:

WHAT I LIKED ABOUT THIS BOOK ....

....

....

....

....

....

MEMORABLE QUOTES ....

....

MY RATING

MY REVIEW ....

....

....

....

No. ○ PAPERBACK ○ HARDBACK ○ EBOOK ○ AUDIOBOOK

BOOK TITLE

AUTHOR .... FICTION ○ NON- FICTION ○

GENRE: DATE STARTED: DATE FINISDHED:

PLOT/SUMMARY ....
....
....
....

SOURCE:

BOUGHT○ LOANED○

FROM: ....

MY FAVORITE CHARACTER WAS ....
....

THINGS I LEARNED:

WHAT I LIKED ABOUT THIS BOOK ....
....
....
....

....
....
....

MEMORABLE QUOTES ....
....
....

MY RATING

MY REVIEW ....
....
....

○ PAPERBACK   ○ HARDBACK   ○ EBOOK   ○ AUDIOBOOK   NO.

BOOK
TITLE

AUTHOR _____   FICTION ○   NON- FICTION ○

GENRE: _____   DATE STARTED: _____   DATE FINISDHED: _____

PLOT/SUMMARY _____
_____
_____
_____
_____

SOURCE:

BOUGHT ○   LOANED ○

FROM: _____

MY FAVORITE CHARACTER WAS _____
_____

THINGS I LEARNED:

WHAT I LIKED ABOUT THIS BOOK _____
_____
_____
_____

_____
_____
_____

MEMORABLE QUOTES _____
_____

MY RATING

MY REVIEW _____
_____
_____

No. ○ PAPERBACK ○ HARDBACK ○ EBOOK ○ AUDIOBOOK

BOOK TITLE

AUTHOR _____ FICTION ○ NON-FICTION ○

GENRE: DATE STARTED: DATE FINISDHED:

PLOT/SUMMARY _____
_____
_____
_____

SOURCE:

BOUGHT ○ LOANED ○

FROM: _____

MY FAVORITE CHARACTER WAS _____
_____

THINGS I LEARNED:

WHAT I LIKED ABOUT THIS BOOK _____
_____
_____
_____

_____
_____
_____

MEMORABLE QUOTES _____
_____
_____

MY RATING

MY REVIEW _____
_____
_____

○ PAPERBACK   ○ HARDBACK   ○ EBOOK   ○ AUDIOBOOK   No.

| BOOK TITLE |

AUTHOR ....   FICTION ○ NON- FICTION ○

GENRE: _____   DATE STARTED: _____   DATE FINISDHED: _____

PLOT/SUMMARY ....
....
....
....
....
....

SOURCE:

BOUGHT ○   LOANED ○

FROM: _____

MY FAVORITE CHARACTER WAS ....
....

THINGS I LEARNED:

WHAT I LIKED ABOUT THIS BOOK ....
....
....
....

MEMORABLE QUOTES ....
....

MY RATING

MY REVIEW ....
....
....
....

No.

○ PAPERBACK   ○ HARDBACK   ○ EBOOK   ○ AUDIOBOOK

BOOK TITLE

AUTHOR .... FICTION ○ NON-FICTION ○

GENRE: DATE STARTED: DATE FINISDHED:

PLOT/SUMMARY

....
....
....
....

MY FAVORITE CHARACTER WAS ....
....

WHAT I LIKED ABOUT THIS BOOK ....
....
....
....

MEMORABLE QUOTES ....
....
....

MY REVIEW

....
....
....

SOURCE:

BOUGHT ○   LOANED ○

FROM: ....

THINGS I LEARNED:

....
....
....

MY RATING

○ PAPERBACK   ○ HARDBACK   ○ EBOOK   ○ AUDIOBOOK | No.

BOOK TITLE

AUTHOR _____ FICTION ○ NON- FICTION ○

GENRE: DATE STARTED: DATE FINISDHED:

PLOT/SUMMARY _____

_____

_____

_____

_____

SOURCE:

BOUGHT ○ LOANED ○

FROM: _ _ _ _ _ _ _

MY FAVORITE CHARACTER WAS _ _ _ _ _ _ _ _ _ _ _ _ _ _ _

_____

THINGS I LEARNED:

WHAT I LIKED ABOUT THIS BOOK _ _ _ _ _ _ _ _ _

_____

_____

_____

MEMORABLE QUOTES _ _ _ _ _ _ _ _ _ _ _ _ _ _ _

_____

MY RATING

MY REVIEW _ _ _ _ _ _ _ _ _ _ _ _ _ _ _ _ _ _ _

_____

_____

No. ○ PAPERBACK   ○ HARDBACK   ○ EBOOK   ○ AUDIOBOOK

BOOK
TITLE

AUTHOR _____   FICTION ○ NON- FICTION ○

GENRE: _____   DATE STARTED: _____   DATE FINISDHED: _____

PLOT/SUMMARY _____
_____
_____
_____

SOURCE:

BOUGHT○ LOANED○
FROM: _____

MY FAVORITE CHARACTER WAS _____
_____

THINGS I LEARNED:
_____
_____
_____

WHAT I LIKED ABOUT THIS BOOK _____
_____
_____
_____

MEMORABLE QUOTES _____
_____
_____

MY REVIEW _____
_____
_____

MY RATING

○ PAPERBACK   ○ HARDBACK   ○ EBOOK   ○ AUDIOBOOK   **No.**

BOOK
TITLE

AUTHOR ....   FICTION ○ NON- FICTION ○

GENRE: DATE STARTED: DATE FINISDHED:

PLOT/SUMMARY ....

....

....

....

....

MY FAVORITE CHARACTER WAS ....

....

WHAT I LIKED ABOUT THIS BOOK ....

....

....

....

MEMORABLE QUOTES ....

....

MY REVIEW ....

....

....

SOURCE:

BOUGHT ○   LOANED ○

FROM: ....

THINGS I LEARNED:

....

....

....

MY RATING

No.

○ PAPERBACK ○ HARDBACK ○ EBOOK ○ AUDIOBOOK

BOOK TITLE

AUTHOR .... FICTION ○ NON-FICTION ○

GENRE: DATE STARTED: DATE FINISDHED:

PLOT/SUMMARY ....

SOURCE:

BOUGHT○ LOANED○

FROM: ....

MY FAVORITE CHARACTER WAS ....

THINGS I LEARNED:

WHAT I LIKED ABOUT THIS BOOK ....

MEMORABLE QUOTES ....

MY RATING

MY REVIEW ....

○ PAPERBACK   ○ HARDBACK   ○ EBOOK   ○ AUDIOBOOK   No.

BOOK
TITLE

AUTHOR ....   FICTION ○   NON- FICTION ○

GENRE: _____   DATE STARTED: _____   DATE FINISDHED: _____

PLOT/SUMMARY ....

SOURCE:

BOUGHT ○   LOANED ○

FROM: ....

MY FAVORITE CHARACTER WAS ....

THINGS I LEARNED:

WHAT I LIKED ABOUT THIS BOOK

MEMORABLE QUOTES ....

MY RATING

MY REVIEW ....

No.

○ PAPERBACK   ○ HARDBACK   ○ EBOOK   ○ AUDIOBOOK

BOOK TITLE

AUTHOR ....   FICTION ○   NON- FICTION ○

GENRE: DATE STARTED: DATE FINISDHED:

PLOT/SUMMARY ....

....

....

....

....

MY FAVORITE CHARACTER WAS ....

....

WHAT I LIKED ABOUT THIS BOOK ....

....

....

....

MEMORABLE QUOTES ....

....

MY REVIEW ....

....

....

....

SOURCE:

BOUGHT ○   LOANED ○

FROM: ....

THINGS I LEARNED:

....

....

....

....

MY RATING

○ PAPERBACK   ○ HARDBACK   ○ EBOOK   ○ AUDIOBOOK   **No.**

BOOK TITLE	

AUTHOR ....   FICTION ○ NON- FICTION ○

GENRE: DATE STARTED: DATE FINISDHED:

PLOT/SUMMARY ....

SOURCE:

BOUGHT ○   LOANED ○

FROM: ....

MY FAVORITE CHARACTER WAS ....

THINGS I LEARNED:

WHAT I LIKED ABOUT THIS BOOK ....

MEMORABLE QUOTES ....

MY RATING

MY REVIEW ....

NO. ○ PAPERBACK   ○ HARDBACK   ○ EBOOK   ○ AUDIOBOOK

BOOK TITLE

AUTHOR _____   FICTION ○ NON- FICTION ○

GENRE: _____   DATE STARTED: _____   DATE FINISDHED: _____

PLOT/SUMMARY _____
_____
_____
_____

SOURCE:

BOUGHT ○ LOANED ○

FROM: _____

MY FAVORITE CHARACTER WAS _____
_____

THINGS I LEARNED:
_____
_____
_____

WHAT I LIKED ABOUT THIS BOOK _____
_____
_____
_____

MEMORABLE QUOTES _____
_____
_____

MY RATING

MY REVIEW _____
_____
_____

○ PAPERBACK   ○ HARDBACK   ○ EBOOK   ○ AUDIOBOOK   **No.**

BOOK
TITLE

AUTHOR _____   FICTION ○ NON- FICTION ○

GENRE: DATE STARTED: DATE FINISDHED:

PLOT/SUMMARY _____

_____

_____

_____

_____

SOURCE:

BOUGHT ○ LOANED ○

FROM: _ _ _ _ _ _ _

MY FAVORITE CHARACTER WAS _____

_____

THINGS I LEARNED:

WHAT I LIKED ABOUT THIS BOOK _____

_____

_____

_____

_____

MEMORABLE QUOTES _____

_____

MY RATING

MY REVIEW _____

_____

_____

NO. ○ PAPERBACK ○ HARDBACK ○ EBOOK ○ AUDIOBOOK

BOOK
TITLE

AUTHOR _____ FICTION ○ NON- FICTION ○

GENRE: DATE STARTED: DATE FINISDHED:

PLOT/SUMMARY _____
_____
_____
_____
_____

SOURCE:

BOUGHT○ LOANED○

FROM: _____

MY FAVORITE CHARACTER WAS _____
_____

THINGS I LEARNED:

WHAT I LIKED ABOUT THIS BOOK _____
_____
_____
_____

MEMORABLE QUOTES _____
_____
_____

MY RATING

MY REVIEW _____
_____
_____

○ PAPERBACK   ○ HARDBACK   ○ EBOOK   ○ AUDIOBOOK   No.

BOOK
TITLE

AUTHOR _____   FICTION ○ NON- FICTION ○

GENRE: DATE STARTED: DATE FINISDHED:

PLOT/SUMMARY _____
_____
_____
_____
_____

SOURCE:

BOUGHT ○ LOANED ○

FROM: _____

MY FAVORITE CHARACTER WAS _____
_____

THINGS I LEARNED:

WHAT I LIKED ABOUT THIS BOOK _____
_____
_____
_____

_____
_____

MEMORABLE QUOTES _____
_____

MY RATING

MY REVIEW _____
_____
_____
_____

No. ○ PAPERBACK   ○ HARDBACK   ○ EBOOK   ○ AUDIOBOOK

BOOK TITLE

AUTHOR .... FICTION ○ NON- FICTION ○

GENRE: DATE STARTED: DATE FINISDHED:

PLOT/SUMMARY ....
....
....
....
....

MY FAVORITE CHARACTER WAS ....
....

WHAT I LIKED ABOUT THIS BOOK ....
....
....
....

MEMORABLE QUOTES ....
....
....

MY REVIEW ....
....
....
....

SOURCE:

BOUGHT ○ LOANED ○

FROM: ....

THINGS I LEARNED:
....
....
....

MY RATING

○ PAPERBACK   ○ HARDBACK   ○ EBOOK   ○ AUDIOBOOK   No.

BOOK TITLE

AUTHOR _____   FICTION ○ NON- FICTION ○

GENRE: DATE STARTED: DATE FINISDHED:

PLOT/SUMMARY _____
_____
_____
_____
_____

SOURCE:

BOUGHT ○ LOANED ○

FROM: _____

MY FAVORITE CHARACTER WAS _____
_____

THINGS I LEARNED:

WHAT I LIKED ABOUT THIS BOOK _____
_____
_____
_____

MEMORABLE QUOTES _____
_____

MY RATING

MY REVIEW _____
_____
_____

No. ○ PAPERBACK ○ HARDBACK ○ EBOOK ○ AUDIOBOOK

BOOK TITLE

AUTHOR .... FICTION ○ NON- FICTION ○

GENRE: DATE STARTED: DATE FINISDHED:

PLOT/SUMMARY

SOURCE:

BOUGHT ○ LOANED ○

FROM: _ _ _ _ _ _ _ _ _

MY FAVORITE CHARACTER WAS _ _ _ _ _ _ _ _

THINGS I LEARNED:

WHAT I LIKED ABOUT THIS BOOK

MEMORABLE QUOTES

MY RATING

MY REVIEW

○ PAPERBACK ○ HARDBACK ○ EBOOK ○ AUDIOBOOK No.

BOOK
TITLE

AUTHOR .... FICTION ○ NON- FICTION ○

GENRE: DATE STARTED: DATE FINISDHED:

PLOT/SUMMARY

SOURCE:

BOUGHT ○ LOANED ○

FROM: ....

MY FAVORITE CHARACTER WAS ....

THINGS I LEARNED:

WHAT I LIKED ABOUT THIS BOOK

MEMORABLE QUOTES

MY RATING

MY REVIEW

No.

○ PAPERBACK ○ HARDBACK ○ EBOOK ○ AUDIOBOOK

BOOK TITLE

AUTHOR _____ FICTION ○ NON- FICTION ○

GENRE: DATE STARTED: DATE FINISDHED:

PLOT/SUMMARY

SOURCE:

BOUGHT ○ LOANED ○

FROM: _ _ _ _ _ _ _

MY FAVORITE CHARACTER WAS _____

THINGS I LEARNED:

WHAT I LIKED ABOUT THIS BOOK _____

MEMORABLE QUOTES _____

MY RATING

MY REVIEW

○ PAPERBACK   ○ HARDBACK   ○ EBOOK   ○ AUDIOBOOK   No.

BOOK TITLE

AUTHOR _____   FICTION ○ NON- FICTION ○

GENRE: _____   DATE STARTED: _____   DATE FINISDHED: _____

PLOT/SUMMARY _____
_____
_____
_____

SOURCE:

BOUGHT ○ LOANED ○

FROM: _ _ _ _ _ _ _

MY FAVORITE CHARACTER WAS _____
_____

THINGS I LEARNED:
_____
_____

WHAT I LIKED ABOUT THIS BOOK _____
_____
_____

MEMORABLE QUOTES _____
_____

MY RATING

MY REVIEW _____
_____
_____

No.

○ PAPERBACK   ○ HARDBACK   ○ EBOOK   ○ AUDIOBOOK

BOOK TITLE

AUTHOR ....   FICTION ○ NON- FICTION ○

GENRE: DATE STARTED: DATE FINISDHED:

PLOT/SUMMARY

SOURCE:

BOUGHT ○ LOANED ○
FROM: ....

MY FAVORITE CHARACTER WAS ....

THINGS I LEARNED:

WHAT I LIKED ABOUT THIS BOOK ....

MEMORABLE QUOTES ....

MY RATING

MY REVIEW

Made in the USA
San Bernardino, CA
03 December 2019